Asleep on the Volcano

The Poetic Landscape of Psychotherapy

Marcus Price

Of all the remarkable poems in this book it is 'The Face' which sums up for me all the aspects of Marcus´s creative and professional life to come. Written when he was still a very small boy, 'The Face' is a profound and visionary poem for one so young. Marcus vividly painted a portrayal of his fearless confrontation with a disturbing illusion that was as actual and vital as that same force he now spreads upon his canvas.

Anne Westley, Artist and Author of Relief Printmaking: a practical printmaking guide for artists and students in the UK, Australia, USA and China

Reading your book, it's clear that you discovered the power of language at a remarkably early age and had the prescience to record it. It's fascinating to see the development of your gift with words. I am left with the feeling that I have spent my life observing the world rather than digesting it.

Your paintings are invigorating! There seems to be a constant struggle between early German Expressionism – Kirchner/ Kandinsky/Beckmann et al – and Pollockian American Abstract Expressionism. Aus dem Sturm strömt Licht!

Steve Stevenson – Film Editor

Marcus Price - an artist whose work feeds the soul, encourages understanding and empathy, gives dark visions a voice and hope. His work affects the world, and those who experience his work, for the better.

Mabelle Pañalver - Poet and Psychotherapist

Art is brave, Marcus says in one of these poems (p. 17). These poems and paintings are brave and visceral, offering "a sense of understanding and acceptance for which the environment is hungry." Sometimes described as "poetic tapestries", these writings draw on dreams of sullen light and unrelenting beauty – often striking, painful and perceptive: "the sheen of your intent" breaks through the "Puddle" revealing the violence of "Subordination", the wit of "Off the Trolley", the despair of "They Took Her."

Natasha Morgan -Author and Gestalt Psychotherapist

ASLEEP ON THE VOLCANO

THE POETIC LANDSCAPE OF PSYCHOTHERAPY

Marcus Price

Written and illustrated by Marcus Price

Published in the UK by EPI Community Publications August 2020

ISBN 978-1-8381-369-0-1

A catalogue record for this book is available from the British Library.

Translation into Italian by Francesca Guiseppina Bascialla (p. 45)

Formatted, printed and bound by www.beamreachuk.co.uk

Thank you to Teresa von Sommaruga Howard and all the members of the art discussion group for encouraging me to publish these works and to my patients who are a constant source of inspiration.

Introduction

Asleep on the Volcano is a collection of creative works. It depicts my own essential disturbance and recovery from working with persons who have suffered injuries of the mind, many of whom have had little choice but to enter psychotherapy from the ruins of their experience. These metaphors for my own journey were crafted in the hours between sessional work with forensic patients, most of whom have been given medication to stabilise or dissipate their symptoms and who live with an uncertainty as to when restrictions on their lives can be lifted, including incarceration. Patients who might struggle with personal histories that for many of us might sound unimaginable, often experience the profound humiliation of a life in tatters.

The Poetic Landscape of Psychotherapy

Poetry is united with psychotherapy in the conveyance of emotion through words. The depth of understanding that Sigmund Freud, the founding father of psychoanalysis, explicates, with his invitations to free floating attention, free association and analysis of the dream, concords to the complexity of poetry. My own poems have been written down and recorded from the age of five. They preserve memories of my emotional being across the years, and to some extent are the preservation of my daydreams. Sometimes I will cite a poem quietly to myself not unlike a musician humming a tune. Whilst music speaks to us of the age it was written (Robert Schumann the Romantic age, Bob Dylan the 1960s) there is also a timelessness in the deeper layers of art, for example, the vibration of string or the shades of tone and shifting rhythms. The early experience of our mother's voice, being rocked in our mother's arms and other such resonances of deeply layered moments are the foundations for empathy and relationships.

The ingredients of poetry are the lifeblood of the human mind and psychotherapy. Sometimes the following poem comes to my mind when a car passes me on a country lane. I wrote it when I was 12 and it brings back memories of my 12-year-old self, but also the roots of my poetic self. Whether I had actually seen a cart on the high street where we lived or not is unclear to me. I am certain that I often listened to the fading traffic as in the 1970s there were substantially fewer cars than nowadays. My mind here quite easily switches from poetic thought to psychotherapy. How busy is the traffic in my patient's life and what was the quality of traffic on his or her journey? Where were the accidents? And where were the spaces to reflect and gather meaning?

Morning

In the morning misty fringe
When sunless light reveals the outlines of colourless objects,
The lorries and cars whilst mumbling, roll forward to view and reveal their complexities.
They rob the morning gift of silence, blending with the twitter of bird or the occasional voices of distant chattering men and women,
But to hear a single engine fade away, to briefly leave a stretch of silence,
Enhances a poet's thought.
Yet if a cart were rumbling there, many a person would stop and stare and listen to the beat of the docile beast with his ears erect, proudly pulling his groom.
I wonder if a poet's mind would spring to life upon this morn?

I was a country boy raised in a
village in Essex that borders Suffolk.
I wrote poems that were inspired by
the countryside that bathes under
the magnificent East Anglian skies.

Sky

A pyramid of rays plaiting the skies mottled edge softly land upon the deep green wood,
A hawk descends to the distant grey,
Again, my head is raised and there I see a mountain,
The sun's descending features shooting down its mighty cliff and piercing its dark belly gold.

Like many children born in the 1960s I was brought up on a diet of war stories that were enacted in our playground games, the preparation to fight fusing developmentally with a sense of my own masculinity. In the following poem there is struggle between two worlds as the ghostly transgenerational trauma of war fuelled my imagination. At the end of the poem the ghost army instantly evaporates at the real touch of the cow rasping my hand with its tongue. This was as instant as a drop of dye dispersing in clear water, 'the dead men dead'. It was written not too far from a disused World War Two aerodrome.

Dead Men

Crumbling earth beneath their feet
Soldiers march horizon deep
Big eyes stare and I stare back, only the cattle know I'm here,
Across these English undulations, reams of ghosts disappear.
And nature waits and nature knows,
The silent rook, the rabbits file along their holes,
The wind gently bows,
All but man.
The cattle huddle by the gate, nervous of my touch.
The sun dazzles, I strain to see the soldiers,
But focus on a floating white fluff and only hear a distant bugle, or a bird.
A hare flies across the field,
The cow rasps my hand,
The dead men, dead.

A similar divide between two worlds, one ghostly and haunting and the other secure can be seen in this even earlier poem, written in my bedroom at primary school age.

The Face

I saw a face one night,
The light was only slight as I stared in bed at the ugly head,
I may have been scared as he glared with a motionless stance.
The thought of fear came nowhere near, his crinkled expressive eyes.
I gripped a feeling that he was concealing the key to another world,
Yet in desperation his one-track soul was aching to pass on a message that he could not tell.
Movement was scarce with me, but my straining eyes could not see one twitch on the face which they glowered,
Then changing to worldly thought, the vision was gone and my dark surroundings changed from gloomy talons to home.
Then a question appeared,
Which world was real?

In these early poems my young mind is aware of a shadow world but is able to return to a safer reality as represented by the cow's tongue and home. This safety for me was embodied in the Essex landscape:

The Oak

The oak like a father stands before scattered survivors
A silver water reflects its light through the branches
and mud scales crystallised like coastal sand rear to the distance,
From a grassy bank to brown mounds harbouring silent foxes.
Then further still to the dreamy oasis, lost from shadow but a rising silhouette from horizons fall,
Source of the sky that stretches to the lonely trees and comforts them,
Tidal from the destination of undercurrent land.

The Forensic Patient

It's interesting that our eyes have sharper vision at their periphery. Sometimes the more we try not to look at something the sharper an image becomes. This is sometimes apparent for the forensic patient who might have the strongest of reasons not to focus on their life's events. The more they lack the capacity to see and face the scenario of their crimes and victimhood, as they always carry both, the more likely they are to re-enact the dreadful defining moments of their lives. Such individuals can convey a sense of being depleted or incomplete in some way. This is not just to do with the drugs they take, illegal or otherwise. It is sometimes due to extreme experiences that have been severed off or deeply buried from consciousness. These experiences are destined to re-surface, sometimes in the form of symptoms in what Sigmund Freud called, 'the return of the repressed' (Freud, 1915d p.154).

It is essential that a psychotherapist manages to allow disturbance to surface in his or her own mind and to survive this process. Reflection is sometimes studiously avoided as it is easy to become too busy for any brief stretches of silence that could enhance a poet's thought and difficult feelings must remain buried. This dangerous situation can be depicted in the metaphor asleep on the volcano.

Pre-Socratic philosophers in the fifth century BC used to meet on volcanoes. Volcanoes were seen as portals into the underworld. The poet and philosopher, Empedocles, was thought to have thrown himself into a volcanic crater believing it would bring him eternal life (Kingsley, 1995). I think the psychotherapist's task is to peer and assist others into peering safely into the volcanic crater, hopefully without sending ourselves insane. There is always potential for an eruption and the histories of forensic patients can sometimes seep into atmospheres like noxious gas.

Psychotherapy for some patients may represent their first encounter with a receptive mind that can tolerate rather than extinguish the heat of their experiences. We can sometimes be aware of layers of harrowing facts about our patients' histories, such as, "You were taken away from your mother as a baby as she was a heroin user. Your stepmother colluded with your stepfather to sexually abuse you. You were taken to a children's institution and also abused there. You were sent to a young offenders' institution at the age of 15 for robbery and fighting". The implications of such histories are far reaching. There may be a difficulty in distinguishing between dream life and the real world, the literal and the symbolic. With such horrific events, nightmares become a waking reality with little refuge from the suffering and little idea of how to receive help. For such patients the experience of an oak tree father, the rasp of a cow's tongue, a secure home, comfort or the valuing of imagination or emotional needs might seem hard to imagine.

Such individuals can present as 'off the wall' or almost totally ungrounded from reality. Other times they may appear to retreat into a grandiose identity whereby they can become the prince of thieves, the chief drug dealer or gang leader. 'Don't mess with me!' The harrowing crimes to which they have resorted can be seen as attempts to resolve inner turmoil, to find relief from the morass of emotional destruction from which they have never managed to separate. This is a search for something real and not just imagined. The atmospheres that pervade such experiences are trapped and sometimes boiling below the surface, leaking like a vaporous gas, and those that come too close for too long can appear intoxicated.

Most patients who present for psychotherapy with severe diagnoses have been in the psychiatric system for a long time and will be taking medication prescribed to them. It's quite possible that psychotherapy would be hard to start without such medical containment. However, it's also possible to use a diagnosis as an excuse to stop thinking, 'He's got that so that's why he behaves in this way', like a high wall that can be forgotten about, as the patient, 'Ain't ever scaling that'. There are many papers and books in psychotherapy that work with patient categorisations, and whilst these are often helpful, individuality can also become lost as patients don the cloaks of their diagnoses and occasionally, what is set out as good intention to elicit truth can become the language of disguise and an excuse never to change.

It is not uncommon for patients to appear as needy children, expressing the early nature of their disturbance in their bodies, in the only way a baby can before the mind has developed verbal dexterity. Regression to such injurious states can be a necessary process in psychotherapy. It was the eminent psychiatrist, DW Winnicott who helpfully informed us that where there is delinquency there is hope (Winnicott, 2011). People with criminal convictions have sometimes convinced themselves of the futility of protest, the transcendent terror of their own anger. Poetry and art are higher forms of protest. The following two poems written in my mid-teens represent my own distress and protest at the institution of school.

Teachers, teachers, a name to caress my brow,
Their heads are big and their hearts are small,
Oh, if I could throw them all in the deepest pool,
I would,
If I had not a human heart.

Certificate Presentation

Let this evening be,
Organised informality,
I'm bored already,
Pickled rows of respectability, in judgment and looking forward to their cigarette, suits, perfumes, ties and façades,
Every other life a wreck,
And crept from many simple homes, the tears, the worries forgot, unknown,
And the note which handshakes tell Englishmen,
Stand proudly before lighted Tory panels,
Live beneficially,
Lie,
Ignore the lesser,
And become in your headmaster phrase, 'Credible'.
And may the world step back in educations praise,
God bless,
Please stay for a cup of coffee.
Clap! Clap! Clap!

Psychotherapy is fundamentally about intimacy and the human need to be in relationships. The desolate cul-de-sac that underpins the contemporary diagnostic expletive, 'narcissism' is profound. The developmental transition between childhood and adulthood is derailed when a young person faces this alone. The next two poems written in my twenties are about surviving feelings of loneliness and alienation.

Breakfast Bagpipes

Naked, Launching melodies from the bathroom,
With breakfast bagpipes,
A Scotsman owned the green expanse,
And when the park met little roads
and little road amassed grey,
The drowsy hum of woken dream
Wrapped in daily course
Hippies, hob-nobblies and delicate child,
Shy from my stare and the bagpipes in my head.

A Day

I opened a box
It smelt of babies and dogs
It had an English dictionary
a Bible and a television.
I went home
Laid in rubble
And watched sunny squares on the floor.
I was led to another box
a stark cold figure of breathing brick
Here inside a lifetime's smell, neat objects, clean carpet, plastic trophies on shiny Formica
I sat down
A foreign body filtering into the television
Nibbling junk food
Trying not to fart
On leaving
The sky was an awaiting world
Red and bleak
Peaceful yet cold
And with falling evening I passed it
Towards the pub.

In our personal psychotherapy most of us can probably resuscitate ourselves drawing on good attention we received as children. In differing degrees, this good experience can be mobilised for our recovery from the parental "fuck up" to paraphrase Philip Larkin. For some though, helpful human contact was sparse or absent and ghostly figures may people their minds in the absence of real human beings. Such patients struggle to work symbolically as there is a lack of what some psychotherapists call an 'as if' quality in the way they relate. This paucity of relational understanding is a result of being treated or used as a concrete feelingless entity in childhood which is now reciprocated in adulthood. Psychotherapists working with such patients need to find ways of understanding their own destructiveness. We can easily become casualties of our own self-importance, self-righteousness or inflated expertise in the face of those for whom life seems ruined and impossible. It is easy to slide into dehumanising attitudes when our own fallibilities are denied. Perhaps for many mental health staff, there is nothing more terrifying than becoming a patient. For the psychotherapist being a patient is obligatory.

It can be tempting to entangle ourselves in tribal rivalries that are stoked by consumerism and the apparent need to defend our positions through research, so much of which has recently been exposed as corrupt (Dalal, 2019). The endeavour to sell ourselves can increasingly take us away from the work we are here to do. We might find ourselves covering the wounds of our patients rather than giving them air so that they might heal. A poem is unlikely to fixate on symptoms that sometimes dominate and freeze our understanding. The making of art is at the core of our human condition and can be a liberation from the strictures of our prescribed roles, the archetypal pull of the therapist – patient relationship. It is the poet who teaches us how to face the imprisonment of our souls.

Art Matures

Art matures
But childhood is closest to the heart.
From an infant's first tear,
Fear is the moon's snookered darkness,
The suspended shock of truth,
Pain's preparation.
Art is brave,
It's safer to blend in crowds like trees
and live entertained to be tamed,
Or does safety lie in ideas beyond ability?
Remember,
You were lost from the Mother's womb and loved by her.

Patients are sometimes unable to find a narrative or even a mind for the disturbances they carry. Such events can sometimes be literally unspeakable. It is this pressure of the unspoken that ripples through the often destructive cycles of their lives. In the psychotherapy space there is a tension between two options, to wake up to the unconscious determinants of our behaviour and work towards the analysis of our dreams, the "Royal Road to the Unconscious" (Sigmund Freud 1900) or wipe out our dreams and embody them in an enactment. I can often see a correlation between processes in my work environment and their deep penetration into my own dream life. This knowledge can be thought about and enrich the supervisory process.

In psychotherapy, a perpetrator can sometimes access their own victimhood in the chain of tragic enactments. Some criminal acts can be recognised as failed and sometimes perverse attempts to break free from an isolated state of mind. Perverse scenarios invade the dream life of psychotherapists and patients alike and these can be experienced as night dreams. The poem can modify these into waking-pictures that can be held and thought about in reflective rhythms. The psychotherapy space is a sort of assisted day-dreaming space. A few poems near the end of this collection 'Alienation and Perversion', 'Dreams' and 'Shocked' were composed directly from recorded sleep dreams sewn together as poetic tapestries.

To Sleep

Reaching into unknown worlds
The curls on the back of your delicate neck
Point inwards and have no external gaze
Innocently they gather as leaves in the old garden gully
Too tired now to bend and sweep the rumpled ground
Nestling in the sullen light of nature's unrelenting beauty
And yet if the tendrils of a ruffled time
Were sending messages to this rhyme
Forbidden as a poet's lisp
Soon all cares shall drift this way to sleep.

Effigy

I awoke to an effigy
Led by the hand
Through a dark canal of dreams, that fell still on the plains of the wild world
In the steps of ancient harmony
A heavy burden
Arose as a row of iron girders that led to our only gate
Our heads lifted to their great power
Looming omnipresent
With small cameras, nipples just out of reach
Our freedom mistaken
But in the subtle seeds of nature's air
Briefly swept from the cold sweat of my mother's body,
In deep breath
Never loved
But at least as this memory hovers
What breath I have
Cannot be taken by the crazy voices
That slaughter peace
And brain us for brief release.

Under The Same Sky

Under the same sky
Flanked by sanguine peace
In a fluffy draft of words
Relative to a delicate moment
Shored by the heaving beaches of nature's frame
Under the same lens of judgement
The same stuttering disbelief
In the basement we sit
Like shackled siblings
Fumbling in the first light
Dribbling our pretence
With food a lust unsatisfied
And love a mumbling crime.

Our Eyes Meet

What movement shapes our frail desires
The bold transitions of your face
The keen breeze that shapes your hair
Where cold ears shadow numb contempt

A will stays here
Whilst all things melt
bones crumble
Breath of the living dead

In putrefying fears that possess our passing
All nerves uncut
Shut into the pale gloom
Where your eyes meet mine

The Golden Mushroom

We gallivanted to the wood
On dreams of fellow women
It was by chance we saw it there
A mushroom made of gold

So rare a find it staggered us
And trusting to our fate
We left it as a shrine
To all the days we'd trundled there, in fellowship entwined

Day by day our mushroom grew
Till there among the leaves
It proudly sprouted several more
So we could gather these

Our mushrooms took us to the stars
To heaven and to hell
Each day we tripped with sodden boots
To look for more among the roots

cont ...

We shouted out to passers by
We've found a mushroom rare!
Some did not believe and others didn't care
It was only fools that foraged in the wasteland that was there

And when the time which suited us
was left to winter's frost
We trusted to another year to find our mushroom rare
Deep down we knew our chance had gone

And now alone I wander
Where once with friend I walked
And mushrooms come and mushrooms go
But never will I see again, a mushroom made of gold

Old Age

The lingering shadows of an evening sun
Slip across
The coarse rusty pages
Of the library that gave and stole your voice
Remarkable still
Is the sheen of your intent.

Death

A skewed note
Misplaced
Unready
On awkward nerve
When all toasted words
Blanket sleeves and woolly gestures
Surge into dreamless anticipation

Death

Yellow tipped dragonfly
Asleep upon the bush, that wavers
as the tremulous old man's hands
Outwitted at last, by the call of birds
That dip to taste your end
A future seen
On the shady path of the echoing green
Where life upon a centuries voice
Falls down to this short moment.

Carry Me

Carry me to the stone
That towers above all mountains
Carry me to the monument of all suffering
I know that you sit poised above the clouds
And rooted in the earth
Like a javelin that slayed all hope
Symbol of symbols
Blunted in earth's fiery mind
Carry me now
Waiting is cruel
Carry me across the field of blood red poppies
To the cold clutch of death.

When I Wake Up

When I wake up
I hope that pictures will illuminate my face
In dappled light
That emulates the cool drench of gentle fountains
And that pain
Will divide itself among the broken leaves
Idly scattered, where bumblebees and buttercups nurture the very core of me
And like a tree
I can stretch unfolded
Desired by the many flowers.

The Short Corridor of Time

Those who are already ghosts
Will not linger when they are dead
But in the shadow of a memory
Locked into the mocking gibbet of this tie
Just out of sight, I will whisper into the ears of strangers

Monument

A child was smacked
A child was beaten
And now as a monument
The ice cream like a fallen steeple
Melts into the hard unforgiving road

Feathers unveil a moving sky
As taken to a lovely place
Denies the road its cruel embrace
And dancing shores the full desire
To cuddle friends beside the fire.

Exile

Derailed in tumbling fate
Aloft this dreadful tribe
A transcendental remnant of your home
Softly speaks through the tip of your finger

Birth

Bludgeoned by a meteorite
That blocks the door
As no emergence from this perpetual baptism
Can free us from the fumes of discontent

No blackbird sung to a sky white frost
Can shake the foundations of this cage
Please pull my frail ankles
So I can be born
On Alpine air of innocent eyes
Convulsed from the underworld of darkness.

Tilt Me Forward

Tilt me forward
From the reminiscence
In your sigh
Dare I seek the sultry heat

The tip toe of desire
Fought and thrashed
Until the slow brushstrokes of regret
Twist divinely in your smile

Pay me now
With stout indifference
Aside from the maelstrom of dangerous wonder
The mistake that gave us birth

Inclinami In Avanti

Inclinami in avanti
dalla reminiscenza
nel tuo sospiro
oserei il caldo afoso

il desiderio in punta di piedi
Combattuto e abbattuto
fino alle lente pennellate di
rimpianto
ruota divinamente nel tuo sorriso

Pagami ora
con forte indifferenza
separatamente dal vortice della
pericolosa meraviglia
L'errore che ci ha dato alla nascita

Despair

We ploughed into the remains of your fleeting nightmare,
Obscure in the rift of smoke,
That congeals in the torment of your fated face
The stolen years stacked in shafts of drunken dust
Blistering, flapping, scrambling, slurries of pointless misery,
Entangled sketches
dumped on inconvenient paper
As the weeds of bureaucratic print
Bleach and depress your direst dreams
Buried long ago in suffocated screams.

Forbidden Tears

Yesterday's coffee sloughed in a poorly fettled mug of reception
Congealed as the bags under your eyes
The future trips itself
As though time were the stone of earth
Neither gone nor to be
But here at last
In the thickening hues of affirmation
Your Shoulders die
To the sullen face
That swells and brims with tears forbidden

Hypno Biker

You're feeling sleepy,
Look deep into the past,
Little green stamps licked into your co-op book,
Deeper
Deeper,
A kick-started motorbike gurgles in winters frost,
Deeper
Engines strain
Deeper,
Engines roar,
Deeper
Distant voices,
Deeper
Deeper,
A winding river full of reeds,
Deeper still,
The blinking eye of a puffed up sparrow,
Awkwardly now,
Trousers split, to the crowd of retribution,

cont ...

In the road, you awake.
I notice the many directions of your broken fingers,
And the huge frantic man
Pumping
Pumping
Helpless, on your corpse.
Further down,
The road
of oil and blood
Your girlfriend was turned to reveal a trendy logo on her top
Flimsy and ripped,
She began to howl.
Further still,
I met the stranger
And lost from the paramedics trembling hand
A bloodied rubber glove rolled past us,
Like a leaf in the breeze,
"I just kept walking" he said,
"I'm a nurse" I replied,
Doubting my words,
There was nothing I could do.

Raw Material

Underneath
The flaky dew of your evasive eyes
A torrential dead river courses like a dreadful army
Abandoned to the dry hammer headed clock
Tock tock tock
Convulsing with your breath
Tock tock
Tick
Did you know?
Did you grow?
Crown
Hammers hanging head
On the rise of silence
And the sinking tock of the thudding block
Stupid stupor frozen lead
In the crypt entombed
With nothing said.

Baptism

The little girl was afraid to move
Unable to peek behind the curtain
Where convinced she was of the baying crowd
And the sea of vengeful eyes
To pillory her like Joan of Arc.
And yet with one feeble step
She fell into the river
To the clapping hands
And the winding rhymes
In the shimmering mist of an ancient sea
And the same crowd forgave her
With eyes of fabled love

Puddle

Glistening in the dying light
On the cold breath of dumb boots
This queer mouldy sludge
Reaps a weak familiar pause
Diminished in the exchange of sun and moon
One part food one part dirt
Frozen once a year
On that spot where I was born

Cry to Sleep

I awoke and saw magnificence
The ocean of providence
Alive upon the puddling beach
With flippers and lilo cracks of thrilling sand
Safe from the deep heaving tide
Prepare me nurse
With your heavy metal buckle
And your goblin feet
Cry to sleep
Cry to sleep

Darling

Darling
Yes dear
Outlandish are the colours of your bruised skin
Cover it now
Lest all will stare
and we will
no longer live happily
under the Emily tree
Or Mummies skirt
that protects us from the boiling sun
and the phantoms that sneak greedily into our flesh.

As the sun briefly tips the corner of your mouth
Radioactive termites
Flop you onto rugged rocks
And squash you between insignificance and God.

Northfield Hospital

Sedation slaps my numb edges
Deep into the last drops of generosity
And into frailty
Till all is lost.

Guilt

Gulp your tablets
Like a burbling wash of corduroy mix
Not knowing which garment
Like toothpaste that
Chokes in particled oblivion
The lungs of giant whales
Whilst declining slowly in this blood-curdling trance
Filthy guilty faces
Pressed in poisoned silt.

Love

Fire! fire!
Illuminate all so that we can love
Not derelict in the fleeting corridors of debasement
But oared in the great waters of life and death
So the thunderous alchemy of our hearts
In the deliberation of your trembling breath
Meets the sweet caress of delicate lips
and explodes into bountiful sleep.

Subordination

Respectfully slung
The decayed apple missed the bin
And rolled beneath the desk
As enters the office ghost
To witness to this mistake
The perfumed spirit of discipled etiquette
Synchronised and divine
To punish the brazen
And disgraced among us
Where dreamy fatigue
And life a stifled task
Is shafted by a boss's beam
If only this once I had not been seen
As I dive to clean to clean to clean.

Off the Trolley

The man behind me must have been born here
He watches for the ritual of the nurses whom he guards
Like the overseer of an execution, his tracing eyes expect precision
This authority he has come to bear
The daily drawing of a perfect square.
Like a mad mechanic in the bonnet of a car, I doze and grip and stare,
What's the other name for that?
Obedient eunuch, spastic muscle, plastic soldier on a rubbish dump,
Ahead full of pills on a trolley full of dust,
Dying to be safe, without trace.
Where's the amulsulptultriptoepinevavarin?
I'm going now, help yourselves.

They Took Her

I really have no clue
Blind
Total incompetence
they took my child
This poem is thin
Pale
No edges
but if it were stretched
It would reach into an unknown space
And maybe there
My baby's face.

On Mountain Steep

On mountain steep
There was a sheep
Who crawled behind a wall
She'd dreamt of chewing daisies
That were growing fair and tall
In time the grinding wind
That growled into a gale
Left the little sheep
Pale and drab
And daisies were a wire of barbs
Till sleep became a slumped farewell
And in the distance rang a bell
Farewell Farewell
Little sheep on mountain steep

Gone Midnight

Gone midnight
They should be back
The unexplained in pasted sweat
Children forfeited to the wind
Scattered seeds on winter soil
Around my heart that pounds so full
Enduring none but the cruel
No space, no forgiveness
Blame or sure
Or fond denial
And when distorted memory bleak
That ran unthinkable flights of pain
Rocks on numb bodies
All feelings now
Vomit before the dawn

Adrift

We may as well let go today
No truth can shame us
for sitting here faultlessly
Adrift
Accept my helpless yawn
and your discerning sigh

As your face leans into your hand
Soft echoes in the mind
We contemplate our break
So completely left behind.

In this land we Phantom meditate
Repeat redoubled doubt
Poise and the unspoken
Ease gently
Towards the shock

Just a Body

Thwarted under heavy dreams
The past a giant ember, blots out all the stars
Deep in decayed memory
Of helpless years gone by
I am just a body
Barely breathing on unformed terrain
The fields are burnt
The trees are felled
This is no man's land
with no faith
No bunker from the withering fire
Hope surges inwards
Our eyes are full of rocks
For tears that cannot pass

Protect us

Protect us warm and snug
From the new,
The ruination of specialness
The betrayal of love
To trust in one another
Change is such a dangerous course
Where need was lost before
The first time that sweet milk was rancid
When mother loved a surly bulk
And pushed me on a wobbly log
Far out to the lonely sea
And now I sit in sheltered sands
Such strangers this way come
To drop their litter on the beach
And ruin this fine land.

Alienation and Perversion

Alienation and Perversion
Came down to the group today
We'd hoped it was a book forgotten
To keep the truth at bay

The raging mob must be a shadow
Greek Myth, Snow White and Peter Pan
Save us love of childhood bliss!
One last disguise, perhaps a kiss
I'm now a patient not a man
It was our group from you I ran.

Dreams

She laid upon a woman and cried the tears of sex
The black clouded bridge of hope that fell upon her mother's house
Her partners children in poison pooled
An auditory allegory of angry that trips upon the fray,
And as we move around our seats our hairs are turning grey.
Sisters we love you although we do not know you,
Unless in strange apperception wrought
The blinding colours of a bomb and death that joins us all.

Pause for the men, Oh pause for the men and let us see their trembling gaiety,
Goodbye upon the crowded guilt, I seldom want to contemplate, the faceless woman all bathed in blood
A child of Dante's past
And the old book of life's dominion get superseded by no opinion.
Relieve us of this nightmare world!
Let's drift upon the play I've never seen,
The brothers love of pastures green

But still the sheep was murdered there.
In life's regrets an hour was lost
And never can it be,
Yet long dispersed we dream again of naked mothers in the shower and king parades like David Gower.

Shocked

Have you been there?
Down the hill
to the river
and the bombed-out town
Hell shaped shaken and split.

To shrink from the architectural ruin
to dreams that scream in the giant hall
Mechanical flesh and death to all.

Spines too weak to lift the coffin
Fingers too limp to pick the lock
As bejewelled spiders our party block
We think no more through fear and shock.

Birds

Gardener of such strange delights
Nimbly tread on this new ground
Where tiny birds just might be found

Fragile birth
Scratched from the rhythm of indecision
Preserved in the curves and rumps of naked fields

Where poets seek a whispered truth
And farmers dream of super yields
What can we muster for this short time?

Obeyance to the wrestling rhyme
Our nature
Dimmed and fraught

On Thursday nights between our doors
As funerals pass
Our limp applause

cont ...

The gaping disbelief
Of choices that fell upon a gentle breeze
And disappeared into the trees

Tremulous as those fallen birds
Our language flits on lonely ground
When life and death just might be found.

The Clinker

Dry in shame the clinker sits
Beneath the ground its builders earned a pretty scene its broken hull beyond their dream.
Once the river lapped your sides and now that saplings soar no rowlock and oar can pride your streamline bows.
The River winds by,
Its banks remember you and flood to say goodbye.

References

Dalal, F., (2019) CBT: The Cognitive Behavioural Tsunami: Managerialism, Politics and the Corruptions of Science. Routledge Taylor and Francis: London.

Freud, S., (1915d). 'Repression', Gay, P., The Freud Reader, Vintage: New York (1995: 568-572)

Freud, S., (1900). The Interpretation of Dreams (translated and edited by Strachey, J., 1955, Basic Books: New York.

Kingsley, P., (1995). *Ancient Philosophy Mystery and Magic, Empedocles and The Pythagorean Tradition*. Clarendon Paperbacks: Oxford.

Winnicott, D. W., (2011). 'The Anti-Social Tendency', *Deprivation and Delinquency*, Routledge: London

Order of Poems by Title

List of Paintings

Marcus Price is a Psychotherapist who lives in the English county of Kent.

He studied Psychoanalytic Psychotherapy at The University of Kent at Canterbury, Group Analysis at the Institute of Group Analysis and Clinical Supervision at the Society of Analytical Psychology.

He has a life-long interest in painting and writing poems although has never formally studied either. He is a member of the Group Analytic Society International and former poetry editor of their newsletter 'Contexts'. He is the founder of The Experiential Psychotherapy Initiative Community, a psychotherapist cooperative that offers affordable professional development courses for healthcare workers.